I0517645

Hebrews

Elevate Jesus

Sarah K. Howley

Contents

Hebrews: Elevate Jesus

Copyright © 2025 Sarah K. Howley

All rights reserved. No part of this publication may be reproduced, distributed, or transmitted in any form or by any means, including photocopying, recording, or other electronic or mechanical methods, without the prior written permission of the author, except in the case of brief quotations and certain other noncommercial uses permitted by copyright law.

Flaming Dove Press
an imprint of
InspiritEncourage LLC
1520 Belle View Blvd #5081
Alexandria, VA 22307
www.inspiritencourage.com

All Scripture quotations, unless otherwise indicated, are taken from the Holy Bible, New International Version®, NIV®. Copyright © 1973,1978, 1984, 2011 by Biblica, Inc.® Used by permission of Zondervan. All rights reserved worldwide. www.zondervan.com. The "NIV" and "New International Version" are trademarks registered in the United States Patent and Trademark Office by Biblica, Inc.®

ISBN 978-1-960793-27-0 (e-pub)
ISBN 978-1-960793-28-7 (paperback)
ISBN 978-1-960793-29-4 (large print)

Printed in the United States of America

Library of Congress Control Number: 2025905460

Welcome

to this study of Hebrews

Hebrews is an epistle written to a group of what we may today call Messianic Jews. They were Israelites who acknowledged Jesus as their savior. It is not known where this group specifically lived or if indeed it was the broader diaspora which was living across the known world. We also are left in the dark as to the author of the letter.

Whoever may have written it, they had two clear themes as they wrote: Christ is greater than anything from the Old Testament and warnings to remain faithful under pressure. With a Jewish background, the rituals and people of the Old Testament were highly revered. This led to much discussion and comparison, with it being paramount to clarify that Jesus was greater than all. The warnings give us an idea that the pressure was ongoing, and it was challenging to continue carrying out the walk with Christ as former Jews. The societal pressure came from both the Romans and the Jews in the Synagogue; both groups encouraged them to renounce Jesus and return to Judaism, so this author wrote that they may remain firm in Christ.

Between allusions, direct quotations, summaries and mentions, the author spent many words on the Old Testament. Arguing that Christ was greater than prophets, angels, law, priesthood, Moses and Joshua, sacrifice and the Old Covenant the author exhorted the hearers to stand strong in their faith.

Given the abundance of references to the Old Testament, only a selection has been included in this study. These selections are intended to highlight the message of the author and to deepen our understanding of connections to the Old Testament in this epistle.

Each session opens with warm-up introductory questions, goes on to a reading from Hebrews and questions related to the passage. Then the study highlights the linked Old Testament passages and questions. Each study session ends with considerations for personal application. Additional tips and suggestions on approaching the study for individuals and groups follow.

Suggestions for Study

This study is designed for individual or small group study and is composed of 9 sessions. It is designed to encourage thought and discussion of the scripture, encouraging individuals and groups seeking God to have conversations about the text. For 'You will seek me and find me when you seek me with all your heart,' as Jeremiah 29:13 says.

General Guidelines for Individual Study

1. Open each session with prayer. Ask God to speak through his Word.

2. Respond to the introductory questions that focus on the theme of the session and what Jesus says in the main reading.

3. Read the passage more than once. Using different translations can offer expanded viewpoints on the meaning of the original text. This study uses the New International Version (NIV) as the basis of questions and quotes. However, any version may be used to provide insight and assist in revealing meaning.

4. This study is designed to offer a starting point for discovery of what God has to say to you through his Word. Because the study looks at how the Old Testament is reflected in the epistles, there are observation and interpretation questions about the readings in Hebrews and then about the links in the Old Testament, as well as comparisons between them passages. These are followed by application questions for personal and group discussion. Writing your responses will provide clarity and focus your thoughts on the verses.

5. Use a Bible dictionary or other reference books to look up any unfamiliar words, places, or names.

General Guidelines for Group Study

1. Come to sessions prepared. Some groups will choose to read and respond ahead of time then gather and discuss together; others will gather to read and discuss together. Before beginning, agree how you would like to proceed so all are prepared.

2. Be an active participant in the group by sharing your thoughts and responses to the questions. Groups often have members who are in different places in their walk with Christ and each perspective should be valued.

3. Listen to each other. Consider the amount of time that is available for all to share and be careful not to dominate the conversation.

4. Be openminded. Participants are encouraged to be open to learning and sharing, even expecting alternate viewpoints. The

Bible serves as the foundation of this study and hearing other perspectives may challenge one's own understanding. When differing views arise, the focus should remain on hearing each other out and encouraging one another to wrestle with difficult passages and concepts rather than building consensus.

5. Maintain confidentiality of the group. For participants to be willing to share and grow, the trust level in the group must be high. Do not share what is shared in the group outside of the group unless permission is given to do so.

6. Expect God to meet you in the study. His Word is living and active (Heb. 4:12) and he is present when we gather in his name (Matt. 18:20).

Introduction

Before beginning the study, rate yourself on your knowledge of the Old Testament and its laws. (1 low, 10 high) Why assign that rank?

What is your current understanding of how Jesus relates to the laws and rituals described in the Old Testament?

Session 1: Superior to the Angels

Hebrews 1:1-2:18

Opening

When is the last time you took time to gaze at the stars. What did you notice? What did it say to you about God?

What do you know of and/or think about angels?

It is difficult to understand how angels could compete in superiority to Christ today. Though there is information in the Bible about angels, many people don't tend to focus much on them. However, the Hebrew scripture noted that the Law of God was accompanied by angels, his messengers. Since the

Law was given "by angels" (Deuteronomy 33:2), the people believed angels were an elevated group. The author of Hebrews acknowledges this tradition of angels being elevated, however teaches that Jesus is greater. This is the first of traditions that the author addressed to ensure Jesus was elevated to his proper place and authority.

Read Hebrews 1:1–2:18.

Reading Questions

The way that God spoke "in the past" and "in these last days" was contrasted in Hebrews 1:1-2. Discuss that contrast?

What had the Son done according to Hebrews 1:2-4?

What were the differences between the Son and the angels as outlined in Hebrews 1:5-13?

What was the purpose of the angels given in verse 14?

Why did the author "not see everything subject to them,"
(Hebrews 2:8)? What did the author see?

The word pioneer in the original Greek was closer to the word
"leader" and perfect did not mean "without blemish", but rather
the verb "to bring to the end goal." How would you write
Hebrews 2:10 in your own words with this insight?

Hebrews 2:11-16 spoke of the family of Jesus. Summarize the
points made in this passage.

Old Testament Links

The letter to the Hebrews is full of quotes from the Old
Testament, directly supporting the point the author wanted to
make. Given the abundance of references, we are unable to study

each one but will seek out those which highlight or explain the message of the author most effectively.

Psalm 2:7 as well as 2 Samuel 7:14 were quoted in Hebrews 1:5. Read Psalm 2 and note what more this Father and Son relationship meant for the hearers of this letter.

Another one of the quoted passages from the reading for this session is Psalm 22:22, saying "I will declare your name to my [brothers and sisters] relations." As you read the full psalm, consider the verses which declare the humanity of the object of the verses, Jesus. Describe the progression of the psalm.

Application

The reminder of God as having "laid the foundation of the earth, and the heavens are the work" of his hands may offer a moment to reflect in awe of the power of our God. Think of two concerns you have at this time. How large are your concerns compared to his creation? Rather than this point of view making your problems small, set your problems in the context that God made you, every cell in your body, and wants you well - whatever concerns you have, concern him. How does this make you feel?

The book of Hebrews opens with an explanation of how God spoke (1:1-2). The second chapter as well reminds us to "pay attention" to what we have heard, to the message (2:1-2). Paying attention implies a cost to the participant. What is the cost you have paid to ensure you hear God and do not drift away?

Session 2: Greater than Moses

Hebrews 3:1-4:13

Opening

How do you find rest? Is it by sleeping, by participating in hobbies, or some other method? Be specific.

What are the various ways that one may "hear" God?

As the first (visible) leader of the Jews, Moses was a popular figure. He was the star of much of early Jewish history. Yet the writer of Hebrews recalled the times that Israel heard from God and He intervened for them, with Moses as spokesperson. Yet that mediated contact with God through Moses was not superior to the direct contact with Jesus that came later. Though Moses was great, Jesus was greater.

Read Hebrews 3:1-4:13.

Reading Questions

What was Moses a witness to?

Use your own words to describe Moses' and Jesus' faithfulness.

What was the consequence given in the warning against unbelief (3:7-11)?

What was it that hardened hearts, according to the passage?

What evidence was given that Jesus was also greater than Joshua?

What "effort to enter that rest" (4:11) should be made, according to the ending verses of the passage?

Old Testament Links

This passage reminded the hearers of the kind of rest that God had promised when the Israelites were to enter the Promised Land. From the passage, it is clear that they did not receive that rest. The author leans on the words of the Psalms to show that rest is still a promise God will fulfill.

Read Psalm 95 and note the verses which were quoted. What did the author of Hebrew's emphasis on "Today" tell you? How did it help distinguish between those who would not enter rest and those who could?

Hebrews 3:16-19 and Psalm 95:8-10 referred to Exodus 17:1-7. What did the Israelites do in that passage? How else could they have responded to the situation?

Application

What lesson(s) can be learned from the Israelites who tested God? What characteristics might we identify as important in the Christian walk when looking back at the Israelite's walk?

The idea of rest took up a significant portion of this session's reading. With the importance given to rest, what "effort" have you made to enter his rest? How much do you enjoy his rest "today"?

Session 3: Appointing The Great High Priest

Hebrews 4:14-6:12

Opening

What are the top three things you would say are the job responsibilities of today's pastor or priest?

Name some of the first things you learned about Jesus or stories you heard about God when you became a believer.

In this passage, the author of Hebrews described the qualifications of the high priest and how Jesus is above this office. The readers of the letter were also reminded to keep the faith and persevere in it while seeking to further their religious teachings. These teachings are strengthened with descriptions of relationship with God, the point of Jesus' coming. While emotion isn't specifically mentioned, the sense of awe in Jesus and his position shines in this passage and contrasts well with the mental stagnancy that can come when we do not seek relationship with God.

Read Hebrews 4:14-6:12.

Reading Questions

What were the reasons the author presented for "holding firmly to the faith professed"?

List the responsibilities of the high priest from the passage.

What reasons were given for Jesus to be appointed high priest (5:5-10)?

What are some of the "milk", or "elementary" teachings the Hebrews needed to move beyond and into maturity?

How did the rain upon the land analogy illustrate the believer falling away?

What was it that God would remember about the Hebrews because he was just?

Old Testament Links

The author turned to a number of Old Testament ideas over the coming several chapters to continue illustrating the superiority of Jesus as Christ over traditions. This session's reading about the high priest is steeped in Old Testament concepts with multiple references to the first books of the Bible. Jesus was presented as superior to these ideas, so as we look into each keep this in mind while reading.

Exodus 37:1-9, 40:17-21 and Leviticus 16:1-17 tell us about the ark as the traditional "throne of grace". Compare these instructions for the ark and the Holy Place, known as the throne of grace in the Old Testament, to the author's instructions in Hebrews 4:16.

Hebrews 5:5-6 directly quote Psalms 2 and 110. Read those psalms and identify the ways this indicates the priest was exalted, rather than exalting himself.

Application

A curtain separated the people from the Holy of Holies where the ark of the covenant was located, also known as the presence of God. Take a moment to ponder what things, actions, or behaviors may be separating you from encountering God.

Hebrews 6:11 encouraged the hearers of the letter to diligence and fully realizing their hope. What hopes has God placed in your heart that are yet to be realized? Write a short prayer asking him to show you the next step to diligently arrive at fulfillment.

Session 4: Power of an Indestructible Life

Hebrews 6:13-8:6

Opening

How do you define a tithe? How would explain the purpose of tithing to someone?

Consider various examples of power in today's world. Consider that of charisma, personality, electricity, emotion, and so on. List examples that you think of.

The letter to the Hebrews gets specific yet manages to remain vague in its descriptions of the priesthood and the ongoing work of Jesus in this passage. Remembering that the purpose of the letter is to establish the superiority of Jesus in all traditions, we can wade through the dense language and vague references to grasp hold of the comparisons and understand the author's root claim.

Read Hebrews 6:13-8:6.

Reading Questions

What was God's promise to Abraham as stated in this passage? What was different about this promise?

What was behind the curtain where Jesus had entered?

How did Melchizedek remain a priest forever?

What were the weaknesses of the high priest as noted in the passage?

What did Jesus living forever result in for believers?

As high priest, what offering did Jesus have?

Old Testament Links

The priesthood was established as part of the Old Covenant, yet here it was set aside for the priesthood of Melchizedek. This priest who is without beginning and without end set forth new criteria for a priest, one who interceded. We were also presented the first account of tithing through this priest.

The account of Melchizedek is found in Genesis 14:1-24. As you read this passage, note the war parties. Why did Abraham make an offering?

What was the relationship between Abraham and Melchizedek? What was the priest's offering?

Application

Look back at your notes about the priesthood. Do you consider Jesus your priest? Note any activities of the priesthood that you have not explored with Jesus. Write a short prayer asking for him to be your priest in all ways.

Jesus' position as priest was established because of the power of his indestructible life. The Greek for "indestructible" literally means "cannot be broken." As Christians, that same life runs through us. How does this indestructible life in you change the perspective of your own life?

Session 5: The Greater Covenant, Hebrews 8:7-9:14

Hebrews 8:7-9:14

Opening

What are the rituals or traditions that you like to participate in most during a church service?

How accepting or averse to change are you? Does it vary by how invested you are in the activity?

This session's reading highlights the superiority of the New Covenant, which is carried out through the blood of Jesus, to the Old Covenant. The contrast of the old and the new, the reasons for establishing a new agreement and how it was better are detailed in this session and the next. The passage may excite participants since we too are part of this better covenant, but it also may incite an awe of God's intention for the heart of his people.

Read Hebrews 8:7-9:14.

Reading Questions

What was the "fault" of the Old Covenant according to the passage?

How did God describe the difference between the Old and New Covenants in Hebrews 8:8-12?

Name three to five regulations of worship under the Old Covenant (9:1-10).

What was the purpose of the blood shed by the High Priests?

How was the blood of Christ different from the blood shed by the Old Testament High Priests?

What other differences were there between the old and new according to the passage?

Old Testament Links

God's intention was always for his people to know and love him, in a reciprocal relationship. This deteriorated significantly from Adam and Eve through the Old Testament period. However, those same texts also recalled this desire for a loving relationship of the heart.

Deuteronomy 6:4-9 and 30:11-16 encouraged involvement of the heart in the Israelites' walk with God, though it was under the Old Covenant. How did this differ from the New Covenant connection of the heart with God?

Isaiah 52:13-53:12 is often cited as referencing the greater sacrifice. Note "how much greater" Christ's sacrifice was as indicated in this passage of Isaiah.

Application

The traditions or rituals of the Old Testament became habit rather than building the relationships they were designed to safeguard. Consider your own relationships with those you see daily or at least weekly and choose two of those relationships. How many routines are involved in those interactions? Note if those routines aid in relationship development or simply maintenance. What one change to those routines (rituals or traditions) could help aid relationship development? What change would introduce them to Christ or encourage them in Christ?

God set out a plan for his people yet had to make changes and sacrifice even his own Son to implement a new plan. What was your reaction the last time there was a change to your plans? What tools do you have, or could you develop, to help adjust to changes?

Session 6: Christ, Our Mediator

Hebrews 9:15-10:18

Opening

Have you written your own will or last testament? What helped you decide to do so, or not yet to complete one?

What do you do when you make mistakes? Are there similar thoughts you have, actions you take, or people you seek for advice?

Christ had to die for us to inherit eternal life through the forgiveness of our sins and for him to open the way to continuous access to and friendship with God. Teachings often focus on Christ's sacrifice for sins. God seemed to focus on the relationship made available by that sacrifice. With the law as only a "shadow of good things to come," the heart and relationship are the key to those good things.

Read Hebrews 9:15-10:18.

Reading Questions

What reason was given for Christ being mediator?

What was the purpose of the shedding of blood by Moses?

What was the difference between the purification carried out by Moses and that by Christ?

Perfect in Hebrews 10:1 means "complete" or "mature". What specifically "made perfect those who draw near to worship"?

What were two results of Christ's sacrifice for believers?

Old Testament Links

Purification in the temple, or to draw near to God in the inner holy of holies, required that one be purified. Today however, we have open access to God without need to stop and purify ourselves. God still seeks to keep us holy and pure, however, this is accomplished in different ways under the New Testament.

Psalm 40:6-8, Psalm 51:13-19 and 1 Samuel 15:22 spoke of animal sacrifices. What was wrong with, or lacking in, the sacrifices? How does that help to understand the superiority of the New Covenant?

Ezekiel 36:25-30 described the promise of restoration for Israel. It too reminded readers of the heart of the relationship. What more can be learned about the New Covenant from this passage? How was the person made holy according to this passage?

Application

The final verse of this session's reading was that sacrifice for sin to be forgiven is no longer necessary. How often do you ask God for forgiveness? Have you ever sought (or thought) to "make it up" to God when you miss the mark? What may drive that kind of thinking?

We have been promised that our heart of stone would be replaced with a heart of flesh. Do you recall the heart of stone that you had? What changes did you undergo to release that heart of stone?

Session 7: Faithful Endurance

Hebrews 10:19-12:3

Opening

Who are two people who have influenced you greatly as a Christian?

What does it mean to have faith?

The author of Hebrews had one major objective in this portion of the letter: God is faithful; He is trustworthy and true. Yet the author didn't catalogue all the people who received what they had been promised. The author listed those who continued to wait for the inheritance promised. Our sight is limited to this world and within the timeframe of our lives; but God sees beyond and faithfully carries out the promises he has given. Even when we don't see it or feel it, God is faithful.

Read Hebrews 10:19-12:3.

Reading Questions

Why could the Hebrew brothers and sisters hearing the letter confidently draw near to God?

What did the readers endure after becoming believers? Describe their attitude.

In chapter 11, verses 4-12, note how 3 to 5 of the individuals demonstrated their faith.

Summarize the results of the faith these individuals had (11:13-16).

The last examples of faithful acts in the reading include several which were acts of obedience. List those people who were said to be faithful through obedience.

Verse 11:40 said, "only together with us would they be made perfect." *Perfect* is again mentioned in Hebrews 12:2. How do these connect to complete the idea presented in Chapter 11?

What solution to weariness did the author give?

Old Testament Links

This session's reading is full of references to people and their lives and actions in the Old Testament. Some appear in children's Bibles with lots of acclaim and others appear to be more antagonists than heroes when their stories are read. Yet each one showed faith. Faith doesn't have a designation of great or small, only our actions portray, or betray, the strength of our faith.

Hebrews 11:27 said, "By faith he left Egypt, not fearing the king's anger..." referred to the account of Moses feeing Egypt after killing an Egyptian and burying him. What was said of Moses and the king in the account in Exodus 2:11-15? What might the author's purpose be in telling the account differently?

Deuteronomy 21:22-23 described suffering on a tree, as noted in Hebrews 12:2. How might this reference have led the Hebrews to exalt Jesus over the other faithful listed in this passage?

Application

Consider your own walk of faith and note two of your own acts of faith. Remember that the acts of faith were not about only grand figures of the Bible, but about how even when struggling they acted in faith at the thought of what God could do.

What encouragement can be taken from the list of faithful figures of the Old Testament? What reminders could believers also keep in mind when considering their own difficult circumstances?

Session 8: True Sons and Daughters, Hebrews 12:4-13:25

Hebrews 12:4-13:25

Opening

What characteristics are needed for someone to do good?

Children are most often disciplined for their behavior; however, adults also receive chastisement and discipline. Name an example or two of discipline adults may receive.

After twelve chapters of explaining Christ's superiority and that of the New Covenant, of which He is mediator, the author turns to the law and relationships that are written on the hearts of the hearers. The author of Hebrews spends their last words on encouraging action from the heart to glorify God.

Read Hebrews 12:4-13:25.

Reading Questions

How were fathers contrasted to God in relation to disciplining their children? What is the purpose of discipline for each, father and God?

List three to four warnings that were given to the readers in Hebrews 12:14-17?

Hebrews 12:18-28 contrasts the mountain of fear and the mountain of joy. Summarize the main points of each mountain.

List three to five exhortations given in Hebrews 13:1-9.

What kinds of sacrifices did the author say were pleasing to God?

What was the content of the final prayer in the letter?

Old Testament Links

Writing to Jews who had converted to Christianity meant that their background made them more familiar with the writings of the Old Testament; many would have even memorized great portions of the Scriptures. Some of the references found in this letter have been clear as quoted, others are more murky. Digging into the texts referenced help today's readers also understand the author's intent to demonstrate that Christ was greater than the Old Covenant and its rituals.

The context of Hebrews 12:15 does not explain the specific "bitter root" as other sins and warnings within the surrounding verses cloud the issue. Deuteronomy 29:16-18 was the only reference in the Scriptures that mentioned a bitter root. What can be understood to be part of the warnings of the author of Hebrews by reading this passage in Deuteronomy?

Jesus "suffered outside the city gate," as the sin offering was burnt outside the city gate. Note Leviticus 16:11-19, 27, 34 (alternately, read verses 1-34). as the law given and compare how Jesus' suffering was superior according to Hebrews 13:11-16.

Application

Consider the list from the first opening question in this session. Which are strengths or characteristics that you possess or find come easy to you? Which could you ask God to grow within you?

Consider the discipline that you (may) have undergone by God. What harvest has it produced? Be specific as to the benefits that have been noted in your life following that discipline.

Conclusion

Throughout the book, the author of Hebrews outlined numerous ways that Jesus and his sacrifice were superior to the Old Testament ways and traditions.

Based on these teachings, how would you describe Jesus' superiority in opening the way to God?

What did you learn about God in this study?

What did you learn about yourself in this study?

Do you believe that Jesus is the Messiah, the Son of God and have you received life in his name? If so, describe the qualities of that life.

If this is the first time that you have answered yes to the call of following Jesus, please reach out to a local church or the author to share of your choice and find support for your new life.

To continue your deep dive into "Seeing the Old Testament in the Epistles", pick up Philippians to continue your study. Find it at your nearest retailer by scanning the QR code today.

Philippians:
Pursue
Christ's
Joy

Also By Sarah K. Howley

Seeing the Old Testament in the Epistles
Ephesians: Experience God's Power
James: Know God's Wisdom
1&2 Thessalonians: Prepare for Christ's Return
Hebrews: Elevate Jesus

Our Trustworthy God: How Much God loves You, Joyfully
Engages with You, and Trusts You

Women of the Old Testament Bible Studies
Hope: A Bible Study of Women in Jesus' Lineage
Faith (coming 2025)
Love (coming 2025)

Alive Again Bible Study on Forgiveness
Alive Again: Find Healing in in Forgiveness
Alive Again Bible Study: Find Healing in Forgiveness
Alive Again Forgiveness Prayer Journal

The Son Reveals the Father
I Am: An 8-Session Study of John

Heart: A 12-Session Study of Luke
Word: An 11-Session Study of Matthew
King: An 8-Session Study of Mark

About the Author

Sarah K. Howley is a Bible teacher, passionate about helping believers grow spiritually and take on the character of Christ. She is the founder of InspiritEncourage, an author, speaker, and trained Christian counselor. She has lived in over five countries on four continents and takes her own espresso wherever she goes. Sarah and her husband support initiatives for feeding the hungry and for expanding access to reading.

You can find Sarah on Facebook and Instagram @inspiritencourage. To book Sarah as a speaker at your next event, please contact her through her website. For weekly encouragement and information on her latest releases, sign up for Sarah's newsletter at InspiritEncourage.com.

InspiritEncourage

www.ingramcontent.com/pod-product-compliance
Lightning Source LLC
Chambersburg PA
CBHW061324120626
46546CB00007B/2668